The Project Management M

Project Risk Management – Simplified!

Michael B Bender

The Project Management Mini-Series

Project Risk Management - Simplified!
1st Edition: July 2013
2nd Edition: November 2013

Please forward comments and suggestions to:
   AllyPublishingGroup@AllyBusiness.com

ISBN-10: 1-940441-00-5
ISBN-13: 978-1-940441-00-9

DEDICATION

To my mother, for all her love, support and wisdom throughout the years … one of the last of the Great Generation!

PREFACE

ABOUT THE SERIES

I specifically designed the Project Management Mini-Series for busy project managers. Project management is a vast topic. While no particular aspect of project management is difficult, mastering all the necessary skills to make a project successful just takes time.

You'll face many issues in your journey to master the discipline; some you'll handle nicely, but some will involve skills that may be new to you. You'll want professional-level answers to specific project management questions quickly. I designed the Project Management Mini-Series for just such occasions.

The books are short, inexpensive, written for professional project managers and designed to be easy-to-read. They get to the point, demonstrate how to apply the skill, they offer tools and techniques and then allow you to get on your way.

The series is not just for new project managers. I include three levels of books, color-coding the levels for quick recognition:

- Simplified! (Hunter Green) for new or novice project managers
- Skilled (Royal Blue) for novice to moderate skill levels
- Advanced (Gold) for more advanced techniques

Some key features I included in the books:

- Templates, forms, charts and checklists with descriptions on how to use them.
- You can download electronic copies of the templates and forms on my company's web site: www.AllyBusiness.com/PMTools/, adjust them for your own style and use them.
- "Tricks of the Trade" is a section I include in each book. This section offers specific techniques I and many of my colleagues used to accomplish the goals and tasks involved in the topic.

I hope you find the series useful. Please feel free to e-mail me with comments and suggestions. I set up a special e-mail address for this series: PM-Mini-Series@AllyBusiness.com.

ABOUT THE BOOK

Project risk management is one of the most misunderstood of the project management disciplines. Perhaps it's because we're not comfortable thinking about the "bad" things that can happen; or perhaps the reason is the concepts are new to us; or maybe it's the constant bombardment from higher-level managers that nothing's supposed to go wrong. It may be simply the highly-academic approach most texts and seminar leaders take when presenting the topic. For whatever the reason, in my travels speaking and conducting seminars, project risk management seems to challenge even the most capable managers and subject matter experts.

Fortunately for us, simple and pragmatic techniques allow us to identify and handle most risks found in projects. You don't need all those equations, probability distributions, and categorizations. Simply sit down with your team, look for traps and potential challenges, figure out which are the greatest concern, then see what you can do about them.

In this book, I try to present project risk management in a simple, easy-to-understand and easy-to-implement light. Throw away the complexities, clear your mind and take a new look at the field.

Project risk management is not only simple, it's incredibly powerful. Seminar attendees who are new to project management frequently ask me what they should master first. My answer: 1) the Work Breakdown Structure (defining the work in the project), 2) writing requirements, and 3) risk management. Why risk management? It's a simple technique that covers all the areas in the field that you might not have mastered yet. It covers stakeholder management, quality, scope creep, out-of-control customers, difficult team members … the list goes on. Whatever your concerns, once you've developed some simple, basic skills in risk management, you can stabilize your projects quickly.

This is why I picked project risk management as the first set of books in the series. I hope you find the book useful.

May all your projects be successful!

ACKNOWLEDGEMENTS

I want to thank my good friend, Ms. Kimi Hirotsu Ziemski for all her help and support and for the inspiration for this book. Also, my good friend, Mr. Gene Spiegle for his inspiration throughout the years.

CONTENTS

1 THE BEAUTY OF RISK

Beautiful? Yes! Project risk is beautiful for three reasons. First, risk is universal; a comprehensive subject from which nothing hides. There are no secret compartments, no lurking dark corners, no undisclosed vaults in project management that escape it. Why is that beautiful? Because, when you learn how to manage risk, there are no areas of the project that can hide from you! Project management is a vast field. Mastering project management takes many years requiring experience in many disciplines: technological, political, supervisory, networking, negotiation, planning, strategizing, team building, the list goes on. It takes many years to master all these different disciplines and to know which one you need to handle different situations. As a new or novice project manager, you may have mastered some of those skills, but not all of them. Those areas where you're still a bit weak, those areas where your team struggles, those flaws in your senior managers, stakeholders, technology, customers, organization; those are the areas that will cause your project to fail. Fortunately, simple and practical risk management can protect you from them all. You may not have mastered work breakdown structures yet, or perhaps you frequently encounter scope creep, or your senior management keeps shuffling resources or they give you unreasonable deadlines; master a few simple risk strategies and you can handle them all!

The second reason project risk management is beautiful is its simplicity. I find it surprising that this topic is so misunderstood. For years I've seen seminar leaders, writers and standards developers take an academic approach to risk management, stressing such useless items as categories of response strategies or making sure we understand which formal process you're in. The Project Management Institute (PMI) defines eight risk strategies in their *Guide to the Project Management Body of Knowledge*[1] (*PMBOK® Guide*) just for prevention alone. They then go and force you to define "workarounds", "secondary risks" and a variety of other useless trivia to pass the Project Management Professional (PMP®[2]) exam. And, no, we don't have to memorize the percentage of events that occur within $\pm$ 1, $\pm$ 2, and $\pm$ 3 standard deviations to two decimal places on the bell curve to be a good risk manager.

If you want to get good at project risk management, throw all those definitions out and take a simple, pragmatic view. Clear your mind. Don't worry about whether your approach is a *mitigation* or a *transfer* strategy. Let's just identify risks, figure out which ones are of real concern, then figure out what to do about them.

The third reason risk is beautiful is the best! Project risk management is one of the best ways to managing up I've ever discovered. Getting senior managers to listen to subordinates has always been difficult. You tell them how many resources you need or how much time you need to get a project done, but they keep cutting resources and schedules. I went through it … everyone does. I've been in project management many years. I've worked on air traffic control systems, helped put satellites into orbit, I worked on the Hubbell space telescope and the United States weather radar system. I then started my 20-year career in project consulting and training. So, I don't say statements like this lightly:

---

[1] *The Guide to the Project Management Body of Knowledge*, 5th Edition, The Project Management Institute, Newtown Square, PA, 2012
[2] PMP is a registered trade mark of the Project Management Institute.

*Master simple project risk management and you'll have
one of your best tools for managing senior management
and other high-level stakeholders.*

I'll show how later in this book.

Our Scope

For this book, we restrict our discussion of risk to the field of project management. Those who handle risks in other fields do things differently. Actuarial risk, for example, deals with insurance policies, where people worry about whether 20-year-olds are better or worse drivers that 70-year-olds. This type of risk is not our concern.

Additionally, we will deal with medium to large-scale projects. If you typically run smaller projects, you can still apply the concepts offered in this text. You simply need to down-scale the tools. I'll offer you assistance with this along the way.

Our scope is clear. We're considering risk management in the project management field, for medium to large-scale projects. Furthermore, this is an entry-level text. Risk management can become very sophisticated. We can model risks, simulate them, apply complex scenario planning, but for almost all risks and for the sake of this book, we restrict ourselves to basic, simple and pragmatic techniques. Other books follow that cover some of these sophisticate techniques for those who discover they enjoy the topic as much as I.

2 WHAT IS PROJECT RISK?

Before I offer a formal definition, you should be aware that modern risk management considers positive risks as well as negative risks. Positive risks we call *opportunities* and negative risks we call *threats*. If this concept is new to you, it might take you some time to adjust; but truthfully, we handle positive risks the same as negative risks. Additionally, we'll see that we must consider opportunities along with threats when determining risk reserves and other factors. For most of our discussions, I'll consider threats. Understand that opportunities do exist in projects and we do handle them the same way.

Risk: A Definition

First, let's define our prey:

> *A risk is an uncertain event or condition that, if it occurs, has a positive or negative effect on one or more project objectives.[3]*

Let's break the definition apart.

A risk may or may not occur. For the mathematicians, the probability that a risk will occur is less than 100% and more than 0%. If it will occur (i.e. if the probability is 100%), then it isn't a risk and

---

[3] Glossary, *PMBOK® Guide*, 5th Edition

we should simply include it in our project. If the risk will not occur (the probability is 0%), then we should not include it in our project and we should not give it any more consideration.

If the risk event occurs, it will affect at least one of the project objectives, specifically: time, cost and scope. So if a risk occurs, it might extend the duration of the project. Another risk might change the project budget. Another risk might change both. Formally, these are the project baselines: the key aspects of the project plan the project manager uses to track and manage the project. Some project managers use other baselines. Some substitute a quality baseline for scope, some have both. Whatever your style, for an event to be considered a risk, it must affect one of the baselines.

Again, scale becomes a consideration. Certainly, every event has some effect on at least one of your baselines. However, if I'm running a ten-month technical project and I find a threat that might slow me down by two hours, I wouldn't consider this a risk as much as a nuisance. If the risk bothers you, place it on the issue log, but let's not bog down our risk analysis with such items. Of course, I sometimes get this wrong. What I thought would be two hours sometimes turns into two days. This improves with experience.

So, a risk is an event that has a probability of occurrence between 0% and 100% that will have an effect on one of my project baselines.

This definition highlights the two key metrics used in risk management: probability and impact. We will employ these throughout our analysis. For almost all our analysis, these two key metrics are all we will need. More sophisticated risk management techniques employ additional metrics, but we'll reserve that discussion for another text.

Triggers

A trigger is an event that either signals a risk's occurrence or warns us it may occur or will occur. Triggers may occur far in advance of the risk event, or just as it occurs. Of course, you'll find triggers after the risk event, but that's too late for us. Ideally, we'd like to find a trigger far in advance of the risk event.

You might remember the period before the 2008 recession. Many middle-class people I've talked to knew we were entering a recession long before it actually hit. In many of my seminars, I ask people what signaled them to the recession. They will frequently cite the housing bubble (it was pretty obvious to many); others cited what the big banks were doing. Personally, I noticed the price of oil jumped from $25/barrel to over $150/barrel in just a few months. Properly-flowing markets just don't behave that way. I knew something awful was about to occur.

Triggers play a key role in risk management. For each risk, I like to find a reliable trigger reasonably far in advance of the risk event. Be careful, if it's too far in advance, it might not be reliable.

Probability and Impact

The two key elements used for measuring risk are probability and impact.

Probability is just that: the likelihood that a risk will occur. Early in our risk analysis, we may simply say the probability is high, medium or low. As our analysis progresses, we'll define an actual percentage. These percentages are usually guesses and probably as inaccurate as our initial high, medium and low estimates; but assigning a number allows us to model the risk if we wish. More on this later.

Impact is the degree that our project changes if the risk occurs. Like probability, early in our analysis we may say that a risk has a high, medium or low impact. Again, like probability, as our analysis progresses, we need to get more detailed. So we'll assign actual numbers to impact. Recall that impact can affect one of three objectives (baselines) in a project: time, cost, or scope. We may determine that a risk will cause a six (6) week delay and cost the project $10,000 if it occurs. A scope risk affects the functionality or appearance of a project deliverable; so the product you're building might not function as originally planned. Note that I do not separate scope from quality, either in this text or in real projects. To me, they are synonymous.

Responses

Our final discussion in this introductory section regards our response strategies. These strategies are how we plan to handle the risk. There are only three: preventive, contingency and acceptance.

Preventive strategies try to reduce the probability and/or impact (for opportunities, we would want to increase the probability and/or impact). We enact preventive strategies before the event occurs. It's a proactive strategy … designed to stay on top of the risk. For example, if I'm driving home and I want to make sure I don't get a flat tire, I might drive more slowly, avoid pot-holes, and make sure my tires are properly inflated before I drive. These are all preventive strategies.

For the record, these are "preventive" strategies, not "preventative" strategies. While you may now find the second term in some newer dictionaries, the former is the correct and preferred form. Knowing this may not make you a better risk manager, but you can show off in front of your friends.

We enact contingency strategies after the risk event occurs. These try to reduce the impact of the event (for opportunities, they try to enhance the event). Continuing with my flat tire analogy, I'll keep a spare tire in my trunk. If I do get a flat, I can change it out for the spare.

We also must consider that response strategies are not free. At a minimum, they absorb time and money. We therefore retain some time and money to enact these strategies as needed. We call these *reserves*. There are two kinds: contingency reserves and management reserves. Contingency reserves belong to the project manager and are designed to handle identified risks. Management reserves do not belong to the project manager and are designed for unidentified risks (surprises). The project manager must ask for management reserve from senior management.

Be careful; don't assume contingency reserves apply only to contingency strategies. Contingency reserves can apply to preventive strategies as well. Contingency reserves are simply a pot of money and extra time you can apply to any risk issue should it trigger. The trigger may be simply an early warning which might cause you to enact a preventive strategy. You would still use contingency reserves for this action.

Risk Register

Throughout your risk analysis, you'll need to capture information about the risk. Any form, table or other instrument you used to capture information about risks is called a risk register. Some are simple, some are complex. You'll find several examples on my company's web site: www.AllyBusiness.com. and many more available throughout the web. Feel free to pick one as a template and modify it to make it work for you. Here's a simple risk register to get you started.

Figure 1: Risk Register

Risk Register - Initial Assessment

		Risk Identification						Qualitiative Analysis				
Risk No	ID	Owner	Description	Category	Root Causes	Response Strategies	Probability	Impact Assessment	Ranking	Additional Analysis	Watch List	Urgent
1									0.00		Y	
2									0.00		Y	
3									0.00		Y	
4									0.00		Y	
5									0.00		Y	
6									0.00		Y	
7									0.00		Y	
8									0.00		Y	
9									0.00		Y	
10									0.00		Y	
11									0.00		Y	

Max Watch List Ranking: 0.2

Categories: Technical, Environmental, Process, Culture, Client, Vendor
Root Cause Enter potential root causes if known
Initial response Enter responses if known
Probability Enter probability as a percent
Impact Enter impact (see Impact Table)
Ranking Computed = Probability X Impact
Additional Computed = "Y" if ranking is greater than Max Watchlist Ranking
Watch List Computed = "Y" if ranking is <= Max Watchlist Ranking
Urgent Enter "Y" if this risk requires immediate attention

While I like the spreadsheet format to ease calculations, it really doesn't give you enough room for text-based data like descriptions or response strategies, etc. Here's a form-based template you might like better. Again, adjust it to work for you.

Figure 2: Risk Register Form

Simplified Risk Register Form

Project: _____   Project ID: _____

Project Goal Statement:

Risk Tracking Number: _____
Owner: _____

Item	
1	**Risk:**
2	**Probability:**
3	**Impact:** Schedule: Cost: Scope:
4	**Preventive Plans:**
5	**Contingency Plans:**
6	**Triggers:**

Risk Owner

Every risk must have a risk owner. No exceptions! If you're running a small project and you're the only team member, then you're the owner. If you have multiple team members, then select the person most qualified to manage the risk (not necessarily the person who identified it – that's just punishing good behavior).

The responsibilities of the risk owner include:

- Ensure the risk analysis is done appropriately
- Watch for triggers
- Enact strategies when appropriate
- Re-evaluate the risk on a regular basis
- Report the status of the risk to appropriate people

Assign the owner as soon as it's appropriate. I like to identify the owner just after we filter the risks (shown later). Selecting an owner before filtering will burden your team with a lot of low-priority risks. Assigning the owner much later can overly-burden you. Once you or your team determines that a risk is important, find an appropriate subject-matter expert and let them run with it.

Once selected, make sure your owners stay on top of their risks. It's easy to forget about risks when you're very busy; then a trigger fires and no one's paying attention; then you find yourself in trouble. Stay on top of them… it's the ultimate definition of *proactive*.

3 STEPS TO MANAGING RISK

I designed this chapter to satisfy two objectives: 1) present a simple, yet very powerful method for handling risks; and 2) create a framework for more advanced risk management.

The Steps

The steps for managing risks are the same whether you're a beginner or highly experienced. The only changes are the specific techniques. I listed the steps below. For the purists, I included the *PMBOK® Guide* process name next to the simplified name.

1. Identify Risks   (Identify Risks)
2. Filter Risks   (Perform Qualitative Risk Analysis)
3. Quantify Risks (Perform Quantitative Risk Analysis)
4. Plan Responses (Plan Risk Responses)
5. Control Risks   (Control Risks)

I'll cover each of these lightly here, then in more detail in the rest of the chapter. As you read the descriptions, you may discover that you can frequently combine many of these steps. It's not unusual, for example, to have someone identify a risk during a meeting; then others will indicate they've already had to handle that risk and they have a workable response strategy. This means you've essentially covered steps 1 – 4 in a matter of minutes. Others risks will require more work.

Identify Risks	This step is as obvious as it looks. Here, we simply want to find all the risks we can. Risk identification is not a single event. It occurs during the entire length of the project, from initial inception through closure. It's one of the very first considerations I make when I get a new project.
Filter Risks	Here, we conduct a very quick assessment of the risk to see if it's worth our time. Some identified risks will have such a small probability of occurrence or so small an impact that they don't warrant any further consideration.
Quantify Risks	Risks with sufficient probability and impact require further analysis. For simplified risk management, just establish a reasonable probability of occurrence along with a cost and schedule impact. For more sophisticated risk analysis, we may model the risk or use simulation techniques. We also find triggers for the risk here and identify the owner.
Plan Responses	This step identifies the actions we'll take to handle the risk. They may include: preventive plans, contingency plans, or just accept the risk.
Control Risks	In this final step, we watch for triggers, re-evaluate the risks on a regular basis, and enact preventive and/or contingency plans as appropriate.

Simplified Techniques Using the Steps

The remainder of the chapter presents simple and very powerful methods for handling risks. I started doing this early in my project management career and found few instances that required analysis beyond what I present here. I don't mean to diminish the power or importance of advanced techniques such as a Monte-Carlo, decision trees or cause-effect diagrams; I just found that involving the right people on your team and staying on top of risks handles almost all situations nicely. As I present these topics, I'll offer examples to show how I did these.

Identify Risks

The primary purpose of this step is simply to get the list of risks. You'll discover that other information about the risk will be readily available during this step, so there's no reason not to capture that information as well. Just don't lose focus of the primary objective.

Risk identification begins the very second you receive the project. The very first steps I perform when I receive a project are (in this order): 1) start the acronym list; 2) create a project plan template that includes sections for both risks and assumptions; 3) start the risk register.

I suspect it's the result of all those difficult projects I've worked, but as someone hands me a project, my mind floods with all sorts of dangers and concerns. Don't just let them float through your mind … write them down. That's how you start the risk register.

The bullets below outline practical and simple techniques for capturing risks. Risk identification is not difficult. The mistake most project managers make is not capturing the information. Someone on your team says something like, *"I'm not sure this technology's going to work the way we want"*.

You respond, *"Well, I'm sure you can solve it, that's why we hired you"*, because some leadership class you took told you that you should appeal to the person's ego and motivate them to work harder. It's wrong. Don't do it. Sit down with the person, analyze the risks together, and then have them take ownership of that risk. That's how you get projects done.

Other risk identification techniques include:

- Meetings and reviews
  Several formal meetings offer excellent opportunities to enhance your risk register. Kickoff meetings are excellent for example. I like kickoff meetings because everyone's in the room, everyone participates so you get risks from all segments of the project. Furthermore, as everyone hears the others' risks, they tend to understand each other better, build comradery and also tend to avoid those risks. This can become a complaint session, so be careful; but with some common sense ground rules, you'll be just fine. I'll present more on this later.

Other useful meetings include: scope reviews, design reviews, phase kickoffs, and most planning meetings.

- Review historical documents from previous projects
  When a risk triggers, it becomes a change. EVERY change that occurs in a project should have been identified as a risk at some point. Your change logs from previous projects are excellent sources of information. Risk registers from previous projects also provide excellent sources of risks for this project. This not only helps you identify risks, but you can also use any analysis (filtering, quantitative analysis, response strategies, etc.) from previous projects.

- Review assumptions
  An assumption is a guess. It's the answer to a question, but we don't know if the answer's right. That's what makes it an assumption. There's an obvious risk associated with every assumption… that the assumption's wrong. Every assumption I capture in a project has an associated risk. NO EXCEPTIONS. When I complete writing the assumption, I immediately turn to the risk section of my project plan and write the associated risk. NO EXCEPTIONS. As soon as I confirm or resolve the assumption, I also resolve the risk. NO EXCEPTIONS. (Did I say NO EXCEPTIONS enough yet?)

- Interviews
  I usually don't conduct formal risk interviews. However, I frequently conduct other interviews (to gather requirements, for example). Before I finish an interview, I simply ask, *"What concerns do you have about this project?"* You'll find the responses are excellent. You can do this with anyone, Vice President to entry-level clerk. It just works well.

All risks go into the risk register, be it simple or complex. Just put them in there. Capture any other information offered (category, root cause, etc.), but don't derail the objective of capturing the risks. There's time for analysis later.

Finally, remember that risks are ubiquitous. They're everywhere! Create a checklist of areas where you typically find risks. PMI calls it a Risk Breakdown Structure (RBS). While I may object to the name, the purpose and use remain excellent.

The purpose of the checklist is to help you ensure you've covered all the bases. Don't let a good risk hide. Find it… anyway you can. Here's a basic RBS to help get you started.

Figure 3: Sample Risk Breakdown Structure (RBS)

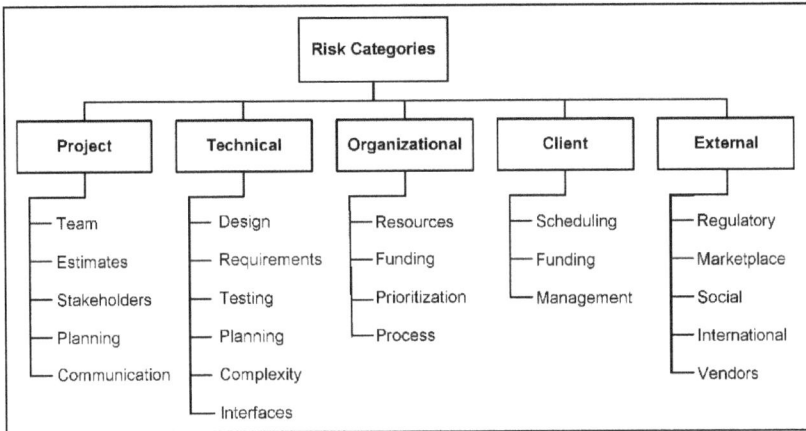

```
                        ┌──────────────────┐
                        │  Risk Categories │
                        └──────────────────┘
     ┌──────────┬───────────┬───────────────┬──────────┬──────────┐
┌─────────┐┌──────────┐┌────────────────┐┌────────┐┌──────────┐
│ Project ││ Technical ││ Organizational ││ Client ││ External │
└─────────┘└──────────┘└────────────────┘└────────┘└──────────┘
 ─ Team      ─ Design     ─ Resources      ─ Scheduling  ─ Regulatory
 ─ Estimates ─ Requirements ─ Funding       ─ Funding     ─ Marketplace
 ─ Stakeholders ─ Testing   ─ Prioritization ─ Management  ─ Social
 ─ Planning  ─ Planning    ─ Process                      ─ International
 ─ Communication ─ Complexity                              ─ Vendors
             ─ Interfaces
```

Filter Risks

Many risks you identify will have a very low probability of occurrence and/or low impact. These offer us little concern and we don't want to waste time on them. Our next step to managing risks involves a quick assessment to determine if further analysis is warranted. I call this *filter risks* or *risk triage*; PMI calls it *Perform Qualitative Risk Analysis*.

The primary metric used in risk analysis is the product of probability and impact. In this step, we call the product the *Risk Score* or *Risk Rank*. Later, when we do a more detailed analysis, we call the product *Expected Monetary Value* or EMV. Using the two terms allows us to differentiate between the early-stage analysis and the more detailed and more accurate analysis that may follow.

Note: You may remember from the previous chapter that impact is the degree that the risk event will change one of the three project baselines. One risk, for example, may only affect the project schedule, while another may affect scope and cost. In this early stage of analysis, we tend not to concern ourselves with such details. The primary reason is that we frequently can trade off scope, time and money. While a risk may affect schedule, we may be able to reduce scope or spend a bit more money to eliminate the schedule impact; we may not. This requires further analysis and we're just not there yet. At this stage, we want a simple impact rating. We'll worry about which of the baselines it affects later.

For this stage, many people will use a High (H), Medium (M) and Low (L) rating for both probability and impact. Go ahead and add Medium-High or Medium-Low to the list if you wish. Multiplying these is less difficult than one might initially imagine. A High probability times a Medium impact yields a Medium-High (MH) ranking. Low times High yields a Medium ranking.

Personally, I prefer a numeric system. I'll use a real probability if available and rate the impact on a scale from zero to ten. Some people use zero to five. It's a matter of style as much as anything else. This numeric system yields a numeric risk ranking. It just works better for me.

Finally, before we conclude this step, categorize the risk if you haven't already done so. You can use the Risk Breakdown Structure (RBS) defined in the *PMBOK® Guide* or create your own from my earlier example. If you're new to risk management you might not see the benefit of this step, but start establishing the habit. You'll appreciate it later.

Record the ranking and category on the form or your risk register. Now take the lower-ranked risks and put them on the side. This is called the *Watch List*. If you use the form style of the risk register, check the box labeled "Watch List" and separate it from the rest of the risks. If you use a spread-sheet style risk register, have a column called "Watch List" and flag the risk. These are the identified risks that offer little concern for our project. We don't ignore the watch list; we keep an eye on it (that's why it's called the watch list), but we don't do further analysis. The others require more of our attention. We'll continue to analyze these in the next step, "Quantify Risks".

Quantify Risks

Now we need to capture the actual metrics of the risk event. If it's only a schedule or cost overrun, identify the actual figure (e.g. six (6) day delay or $10,000 overrun). For events that impact scope, state the effects on the product requirements.

You don't need to be fancy and try to keep the politics out of it. Simply state what will or won't happen if the risk occurs.

Next, firm up the probability of occurrence. Make it numeric if you haven't already done so. If you used a percentage number in the previous step as I do, make sure it's accurate.

Once you have the numbers, you can multiply probability by impact. The resulting number is called *Expected Monetary Value* (EMV), even if it's a schedule impact. EMV becomes the basis for your project's contingency reserves.

Example: you're building a house in the spring. Typically, the general contractor will allocate about 3 days a month for weather delays, but the long-term forecasts indicate this spring will be wetter than normal. You might identify a schedule risk for weather. You go on the National Oceanic and Atmospheric Administration (NOAA)'s web site for some historical data and their forecasts. You estimate a 40% probability that you'll get an additional 12 days of delay over the few months that your project runs. For this risk alone, your EMV is:

Equation 1: Expected Monetary Value

EMV = 12 Days X 40% = 4.8 Days

Scope risks require a bit more analysis. Recall that I don't separate scope from quality. A scope risk is one where you won't meet requirements. In other words, the resulting products won't function or appear exactly the way you planned. For scope risks I simply describe the revised functionality.

Example: Your project involves building a web site that includes a complex data base look-up feature. Your management legitimately demands that the site be operational by a particular date to coordinate with a new product rollout. Your risk is that you won't be able to finish the data base look-up feature in time. While this would normally be a schedule risk, you'd have to describe it as a scope risk since you can't delay the project. In this situation, I'd have my team determine the amount of functionality they thought they could incorporate by that date and describe the rest of the functionality as *at risk*.

NOTE: You can't compute EMV for scope risks unless you establish a plan to fix the issue, but that's the next section.

Plan Responses

Perhaps one of the greatest mistakes I see project managers make is they simply don't follow through on their risk analysis. They identify the risks, filter them, and then ignore them. The true power and beauty of risk management is developing the response strategy. Plan how you will handle the risk. You can change the work plan, use different resources, find an alternative and less risky solution; but do something!

There are three kinds of response strategies: preventive, contingency and acceptance. Don't worry about any further categorization. For most risks, sophistication is both unnecessary and inefficient. Simply get the team together and ask them for strategies to mitigate the risk or recover from it. If more sophistication is required, find appropriate subject-matter experts and have them do the analysis. They should know how. Standard problem-solving techniques work well; Failure Mode and Effect Analysis (FMEA) or other techniques may be required, but you usually don't have to over-think it.

Control Risks

I set up two kinds of schedule events to control risks. First, take the triggers for my major risks (anything not on the watch list) and place them as milestones in the project schedule. Use these milestones to review the associated risk. Second, have a regular schedule where you review the risks. I usually do this at the end of the month as I create the monthly status report for senior management. I find this point convenient as I'll include up-coming risks in that report. This helps me manage their expectations.

At each of these events, review appropriate risks. PMI calls this "Risk Reassessment". Reassessment involves altering the probability, impact, or may require you to activate a response strategy. Some risks might disappear while others may be imminent. Adjust your risk register and contingency reserves appropriately.

Risks and Change Management

This is important! When a risk triggers, it becomes a change. It's not an issue or a problem, it's a change! It affects a baseline. When an event affects a baseline, it's a change not an issue. It goes through your change management process.

When I define my change management process, I allow the project manager to approve certain changes. Specifically, this includes identified risks as long as contingency money (and time) is available. I don't need the approval of a Change Control Board (CCB) or sponsor to handle an identified risk that triggers, but I DO want to report it as a change. Also, my change categories align with my risk categories. This allows me to track changes against risks for future projects.

4 RESPONSE STRATEGIES

This chapter presents basic risk response strategies. There are three types: preventive, contingency and acceptance as described below:

Preventive   Preventive strategies occur before the risk event. You can simply modify your plan ahead of time, or you can wait for a trigger that signals the risk may be imminent. Preventive plans reduce the probability or impact of the risk event.

Contingency   Enact contingency plans after the risk occurs. Contingency strategies are your recovery procedures.

Acceptance   Acceptance is a strategy, contrary to popular belief. It simply states that you're willing to accept the consequences of the risk.

I describe each in more detail in the following sections.

Preventive Strategies

Preventive strategies attempt to either stop the risk from occurring entirely (i.e. reduce the probability to zero), reduce the probability (but not to zero) or reduce the impact of the risk if it occurs.

The key to successful prevention is to review your work plan and see if there's another way to accomplish your project that circumvents the risk. Perhaps you're designing a power supply for a system you're building and your electrical engineering department is very tight on resources. You've identified a risk that the power supply will be late because of resource constraints. One solution would be to buy an existing power supply from an outside supplier. This strategy eliminates the resource risk. It may add secondary risks, such as cost overruns, but you'll get your power supply in time.

Preventive strategies can also reduce the probability and/or impact, but not to zero. Using the example above, I might work with the department manager to see when they have a quiet period; then see if I can adjust the project plan so the design occurs in that period. You might also be willing to pay overtime if necessary to get the power supply completed in a timely manner. These reduce the probability, but not to zero.

Typical preventive strategies include:

- Change the Work Plan
  Change the work plan to avoid or reduce the risk. For example, instead of facing a risk of designing a new component, use an existing component that already works.

- Outsource
  Outsource either the work or the item you need. This is one of the most common risk mitigation strategies. You can outsource simply to augment resources (reduce resource risk), hire expertise (reduce technical risk), save time (reduce schedule risk), or save money (reduce cost risk). I know project managers that outsourced to avoid working with dysfunctional internal departments.

- Research
  I use this technique frequently for high-technology projects. When you're dealing with new and risky technology, establish research work early in the project to eliminate the unknowns or risky areas.

- Prototype
  This is a common technique to handle clients or stakeholders who don't quite know what they want. Let them see it, touch it, and play with it. Show them how the prototype relates to the project's requirements. Prototyping also works to reduce technology risks. These are called *proof-of-concept* prototypes.

- Tools
  Often overlooked, getting better tools in place for your team is an excellent strategy for reducing risk.

- Insurance and Bonds
  This technique is more common than most project managers realize. Construction projects of sufficient size (usually $50,000 or more) require payment bonds and performance bonds. The payment bonds ensure the contractor pays their sub-contractors and the performance bond kicks in if the contractor goes bankrupt or simply skips town.
  Consultants frequently obtain errors and omissions insurance for larger contracts.
  In the early 1980's, I worked with RCA on a satellite launch (SatCom 3R). The R stood for "replacement". SatCom 3 blew up in space (for you science buffs, the Apogee Kick Motor (AKM) seals leaked and fried the satellite). Lloyds of London, a major insurance firm, paid for a replacement satellite, replacement launch and two years of lost business.

Preventive strategies likely will affect time and cost, so include this in the plan. Of course, the time and cost impact of the preventive strategy may be prohibitive, so you may have to just accept the risk.

Contingency Strategies

Contingency plans take place after the risk occurs. There are no formal or standard approaches to contingency planning. The secret for contingency planning is simply that … plan for it. Get the team together and determine what you'll do if the risk occurs. Perhaps you're working with a new vendor (always a risk) and you're concerned about a short schedule delay. You might simply plan for overtime or plan to add more people to the project to make up the difference. Maybe you're designing a complex component for your new system and you're worried it might not be ready in time for a trade show. You might be able to use a pre-existing component for that show.

Communicating your contingency plans to your stakeholders is just as important as developing them. When a (negative) risk fires it upsets everyone. If you've communicated with your stakeholders and you have a contingency plan in place, they'll know you're on top of it and you're doing your job. COMMUNICATE!

Like preventive strategies, contingency plans cost time and money. Ideally, you'll have enough contingency reserve to handle the risk.

Preventive + Contingency

It's perfectly okay to combine both strategies. You might select a contingency plan for a particular risk. To simplify the contingency plan, you put things in place ahead of time. If your risk is getting a flat tire, you'll have a spare. Putting the spare tire and car jack in your truck is a preventive strategy that reduces the impact of getting a flat tire. Then, when you get a flat, you change the tire. That's your contingency plan.

Perhaps your risk is that a key component won't work and you have an alternative part. You might get the alternative part ready and ensure your new system will work with it just in case the key component fails.

Maybe your risk is a key team member gets sick or gets another job; you'll identify a backup team member to take over in their place. You have them work with the key team member, attend their meetings and keep them informed on their activities just in case. Note that this is VERY common for key personnel in professionally-run projects.

As always, ensure you account for the time and money for your response strategies.

Where should I put my contingency time and money?

Project managers frequently ask me where to put the contingency reserves. There are two answers depending on your senior management. Some (less sophisticated) managers just want things to go smoothly and can't handle the concept of risk. For those managers, I bury all the contingency inside the project. I'll show you where shortly.

For more sophisticated senior management - those who understand risk and allow their project managers to handle it - I usually like to bury about half the contingency reserves inside the project and keep the other half as a general fund. This is a good habit to establish. When you start running larger and more formal projects, you'll learn that there are rules regarding moving contingency reserves. Sometimes you can move reserves from one task to another, other times you can't. They're called *allocated* and *unallocated* reserves. While these rules are beyond the scope of this book, it's important that you start good habits now that will carry you forward.

It probably won't surprise you that you put contingency reserves in high-risk areas. If a particular work package has some technology risk, allocate some contingency time and money specifically to that work package. I also like to allocate a little reserve for customer reviews, especially if I have a client who doesn't understand their project.

Source and sink nodes also make excellent places to put schedule reserves. A source node is a task with many successors (tasks that follow immediately after it - see Figure 4). A typical example is completing a design. Once the design completes, you can build a lot of components in parallel, so you'll have a lot of resources scheduled just as the design finishes. If the design is late, your resources will have nothing to do. In the example below, *Design System* is the source node.

Figure 4: Example of a Source Node

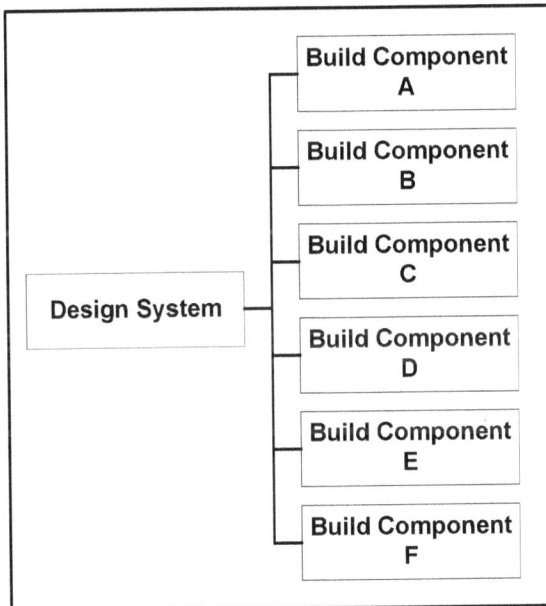

Sink nodes are the opposite: you have many tasks feeding into one (see Figure 5). If any of the preceding tasks are late, the successor is late. This is a good location to insert some schedule reserves. Note further that this architecture is a bad plan (for more than just the schedule risk). Integrate only 2 or 3 components at a time; this significantly reduces both schedule and technical risks. In Figure 5, *Integrate System* is the sink node.

Figure 5: Example of a Sink Node

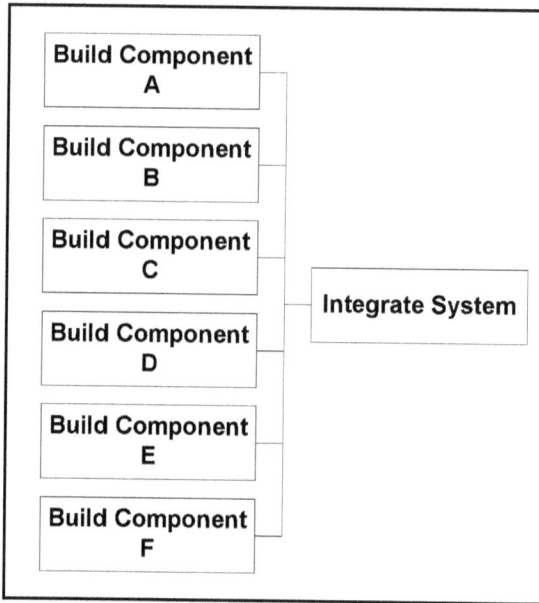

5 TRICKS OF THE TRADE

At this point you know the basic steps for handling risks. To aid you with getting more comfortable in this field, I describe my favorite techniques below. Practice them, adjust them, make them work for you. For several, I offer alternatives. Invent a way that you and your team find useful.

Brainstorming Light

Brainstorming is one of the most common methods for identifying risks, identifying response strategies or contingency plans.

Note that what most people call brainstorming really isn't formal brainstorming, I call it *brainstorming light*. Formal brainstorming is a very formal process. In brainstorming, you end up with hundreds of ideas. In formal brainstorming, no one's allowed to comment on any ideas (including the facilitator), duplicates are allowed and you run it until the group is exhausted. I've run formal brainstorming sessions that lasted for over 45 minutes. Following brainstorming, you run an exercise called *affinity diagramming* to sort and organize the ideas. These techniques are quite useful, but few people run them.

What most people do I call brainstorming light. Here, (as in formal brainstorming) we gather our team. We clearly define the goal of the session, obtain consensus on the goal and write it on the flip chart or whiteboard to help keep the team's focus. Then we simply ask for the ideas. Unlike formal brainstorming, I group similar ideas, filter duplicates and provide a little direction. In brainstorming light, I typically end up with about 20 ideas, not hundreds.

The trick with brainstorming light, since we do direct the group, is the facilitator MUST be unbiased if not independent to the project. This is difficult for most project managers. It's not a bad idea to have a colleague outside the project run them for you (you can reciprocate and run his/hers). Once you have your list of risks or response strategies, use *Nominal Group Technique* to prioritize the list. I describe this technique in the next section.

Nominal Group Technique

Nominal Group Technique (NGT) is actually a collection of methods for prioritizing and sorting relatively small lists. You run a brainstorming light session and generate some 20 risks or response strategies. Now you want to determine which of these the group thinks is the best, or highest priority, or most important, etc. It's an extremely useful technique, it produces great results and gets team consensus. There are also many different ways to run it, so it adapts easily to different situations.

NGT basically is any group voting method. For my examples, let's assume we have 18 response strategies for an identified risk. One method I'll use to rank these strategies is to have the individuals in the group select the 10 strategies they think are the best (statisticians tell me the correct number to select is ½ the total number of items in the list plus 1). I have them write those strategies down on a piece of paper. I simply go down the list, one by one, and if the item I'm pointing to is on their list of 10, they raise their hands and I count hands. You'll find you get several items with high counts, several with medium counts and several with low counts. According to your group, the high counts are your best strategies.

I commonly use this method to filter risks for smaller projects. Get the team together and conduct a brainstorming light session to identify 20 - 25 risks. Then, explain that you want to find the risks which require the most attention. These are the risks with medium-to-high probability and medium-to-high impact. Have the individuals identify the risks that require the most attention and run the session as I described above. The high-count risks will go onto quantitative analysis and the rest go on the watch list.

Another voting method is simply give the individuals in the group a set of dot stickers they can place on any items they want. In the above example, assuming I have 20 risks, I might give each person 11 (½ the total number plus 1) dots. They go up to the board and place the dots on the items they think are the best. They can put all 11 dots on one item if they want. Note that I always carry an envelope with orange dots with me just in case I need to run an NGT in a seminar or consulting session.

If you have strong personalities in the group or other political issues, you should consider a secret ballot. For example, if there's a senior-level manager in the room, people will play to the manager rather than offer true responses. Have them list the items on a piece of paper and pass them forward.

You can estimate probabilities with this technique as well. Have everyone write their estimate for the probability for the risk on a piece of paper and pass them forward. You average the numbers and use that as your probability estimate.

In some of my advanced project management seminars, I'll have the groups run an NGT to estimate the probability (high, medium or low), then a second NGT to determine impact (high, medium or low), then multiply them to determine the risk score. They now use these to filter their risks for their case study.

Delphi Technique

Delphi technique is one of my favorite techniques for generating ideas or obtaining consensus. I run it frequently. Delphi originally was designed for formal, world-class research studies. The Rand Corporation, a world-class think-tank started running Delphi's in the 1960's. To run one, you gather a group of experts to determine their opinion or obtain consensus. The problem with gathering a group of experts is that egos tend get in the way. So, Delphi technique eliminates this by keeping the members of the group anonymous.

Today, you can do this quite easily using blind carbon copy (BCC) e-mails. I select a group of people I want for the study and create an e-mail group. I generate an e-mail with the question I want answered and BCC the group. I collect the responses, paraphrase and summarize. Paraphrasing and summarizing is important to retain anonymity. I generate the next e-mail showing the progress to date and ask for another review. Each one of these cycles is called a *Delphi Round*. You'll have consensus usually in about 3 – 4 rounds. Many of my participants don't even know they're in a Delphi.

At the time of this writing, I'm currently running one to see what books I should write for this risk management series.

6 RISK'S GREATEST BEAUTY

Perhaps the best benefit of managing risks goes beyond managing your project. To me, the best benefit of risk is managing my stakeholders, including clients and senior management. I found it's an excellent method to manage up. The next few sections describe how I like to use risks to manage stakeholder expectations and educate my senior management about projects.

Rule 1: No Surprises

No one wants bad things to happen. But, if they're going to, it's better to be on top of them. Don't hide your risk register. Tell your stakeholders your concerns and what you plan to do about them. At first, unless they were trained in project management, they won't get it. Don't worry, they will!

So, you smartly identify resource risks in your project charter and risk register. Your team is pulled in 20 different directions, working on multiple other projects and frequently interrupted with "other duties as assigned". You make the following statement in your project charter or risk register:

> *"Project estimates are based on team availability. If the team members are redirected to other projects or activities, project delays and overruns will result."*

If your managers are like most I've seen, they'll ignore this statement. At some later time, they'll pull your resources away from you. Then, you'll write up a change order declaring a project slip. Then, you'll be called into someone's office for a good scolding. Then … you get to say "I told you so".

They won't like it. They'll be angry. Hold your ground. This victory is yours. Note that I've done this on several occasions successfully. I have my style. You need to find your own style … do things your way, but find a way. More on this in the next section.

Negotiating with Senior Management

The first and most important trick to negotiate with senior management and other key high-level stakeholders is Rule 1: No Surprises. Communicate your risks in advance and show you're on top of them. You show you're on top of them by conveying the response strategies. This is important! I found that communicating risks without a response strategy shows you're not in control, your afraid – it's whining. Communicating a risk with a response strategy shows you're a manager.

You're planning your project. Like all projects, senior management wants this done FAST! You identify a resource risk as we did in the previous section. For this example, we'll use a bit more sophistication. We identify the risk regarding our two key team members, let's call them Jane and Bob. Your risk register indicates that they are critical to progress and if they're pulled off your project, you'll take a day-for-day slip. Probability: high. You review the project plan with your management. During the session, you convey the risk that Jane and Bob are critical and need to stay on the project.

Later, you're running your project. Some senior manager comes to steal Jane to handle some other issue. At this point, your negotiation stance is solid. You've already conveyed the risk. You indicate you'll take a day-for-day slip of Jane leaves the project. Your manager won't like it, but there's no wiggle room. The ball's in their court. They have to make a decision, *"Do I take Jane and cause this project to slip, or do I find other resources?"* If they decide to take Jane, you fill out your change management form, you declare the project slip and continue merrily on your way.

I don't care if a project slips as long as my management agrees to the slip. That's their decision, not mine. My job is to convey the result of their decisions, not to make the decision. If they have a legitimately higher-priority issue afoot, then take my resources; but don't punish me for the project slippage. Publish a new schedule and manage the project to the new schedule.

Something else I've noticed regarding this situation. Senior managers don't like disturbing well-managed projects. They'd rather disturb unmanaged projects. If you show you're on top of your project, senior managers tend to leave you alone. They'd rather grab a resource that's being mismanaged anyway. Wouldn't you?

Managing Up

We've now set the stage for managing up. Understand, it's not my position that senior managers are stupid, uneducated, or otherwise incompetent or corrupt (well, mostly). Management classes, MBA programs and other management training avenues classically teach process-based concepts, not project-based concepts. We as project managers face this problem daily. Sadly, since universities won't teach this stuff, we'll have to do it on-the-job.

So, how do I manage up? Well, I've already set the stage. It's based on demonstrating the cause-effect relationships in decision-making. Once senior management understands the cause-effect relationship, they can make better decisions.

In the last section, we played out a scenario where a critical resource was pulled from a project. We showed our management the relationship between resource allocation and project schedules. Note that when I identified the risk of losing Jane or Bob, I didn't identify everyone on the project, just my key people. I didn't get greedy, but I did show a clear relationship between Jane and Bob's involvement and the project schedule.

More importantly… I've shown that I'm a good manager, that I understand this relationship. My management will now start to respect what I say. Since they saw the project slippage in this project, the next time I identify a resource risk, they'll tend to listen a bit better. The absolute best scenario is that on the next project, I get to keep Jane and Bob and bring the project in on time! There's no better proof of this cause-effect relationship than that!

Once I've established my reputation, I can continue to use risk as a managing-up tool. You can use it for technology risks where managers don't understand the complexity of the technology. You can use it for organizational risks where political issues delay critical approvals. You can even use it to improve the overall quality of project work. Risk allows you to identify cause-and-effect relationships in advance and prove those relationships. So, to manage up:

- Identify true and accurate risks (as you should anyway)
- Communicate those risks to appropriate stakeholders and managers (as you should anyway) showing clear relationship between the risk and results (cause-effect).
- As managers make decisions, restate the relationship between the risk and results (as you should anyway)
- After the decision, show how the relationship played out (as you should anyway)

As with all my examples, I show the style I used to get things done. You need to work out your own style, but I hope this demonstration helps you be a more successful project manager.

7 SUMMARY

I hope you now understand why I think risk management is beautiful. It's extremely powerful. It solidifies and stabilizes your projects. It helps maintain stakeholder expectations. You can even learn how to use it to manage up.

It's also one of the simplest disciplines in project management. Identify risks, filter them, quantify them and determine what you plan to do about them. And you, as project manager, don't even need to make these decisions ... that's what you have a team for. Let your subject matter experts do their job.

In this book, I presented the key steps in risk management. This book also offers simple, yet powerful methods for handling risks. If you're new at risk management, you now have enough knowledge to handle almost all risks. Now it's time to practice. Get used to the forms and risk register. Change them to make them work for you. Define your categories, and as you see problems, adjust your categories. Get comfortable with the process. It's not difficult; you just have to do it.

The key conditions you should look for:

- The information in the risk register should flow. You should be able to pick up a risk register form you wrote six months ago and completely understand the risks.

- Upper-level stakeholders should also understand the risks. While they may not completely understand the technology involved, they should understand the key aspects of the risks, why you selected particular response strategies and how you intend to monitor the risk.

- Categories should be stable and understandable. They should also track directly to the change management categories. Your categories are solid when you start seeing trends and patterns.

- Your response strategies should hold up. If you're new at risk management, you might discover that what you planned as a response strategy won't really work when the risk actually fires. Don't give up or lose hope, just learn from the incident. It won't take long. Soon, your response strategies will be solid and handle the risk events nicely.

- Finally, at the beginning, you'll find some identified risks falling through the cracks. This is a monitoring issue. Make sure every risk has an appropriate owner and tighten up your rigger on your regularly-scheduled reassessments and confirm your milestones. Like the previous conditions, this one won't take long to master as long as you stay on top of it.

Once you're comfortable at this level, move on to the next books and we'll take it to the next level.

Good luck, and may all your projects be successful!

ABOUT THE AUTHOR

Mr. Bender, president of Ally Strategic Partners, Ltd., is an accomplished speaker, author and seminar leader in the business management field. Specializing in all areas of strategic planning, work flow management and resource management, Mr. Bender is a frequent speaker for: Rutgers University Business School, DeVry University – Becker Professional Education, Global Knowledge, American Management Association and many other companies, organizations and universities. Mr. Bender's keynote speeches specialize in advanced concepts in resource management across strategic plans, programs and portfolios for industry, non-profit, educational and government sectors.

Mr. Bender began his career in high-technology fields. Specializing in computer systems development, Mr. Bender worked both as a subject matter expert and project manager on such projects as: the Hubbell Space Telescope, the US weather radar system, air traffic control systems in three continents, satellite launches, cable television automation systems and many other technology-based projects. Through this experience, Mr. Bender developed his unique skills in advanced program management, resource allocation and strategic planning.

Mr. Bender's additional books in project management include:

- *A Manager's Guide to Project Management*, Financial Times Press, 2010
- *Setting Goals and Expectations*, Virtual Bookworm Publishing, 2004

For more information, visit Ally's web site at www.AllyBusiness.com.

www.ingramcontent.com/pod-product-compliance
Lightning Source LLC
Chambersburg PA
CBHW071336200326
41520CB00013B/3005